salmonpoetry

Diverse Voices from Ireland and the World

the arts council an chomhairle ealaíon | funding literature

Thin Lines
Emer Fallon

Published in 2023 by
Salmon Poetry
Cliffs of Moher, County Clare, Ireland
Website: www.salmonpoetry.com
Email: info@salmonpoetry.com

Copyright © Emer Fallon, 2023

ISBN 978-1-915022-42-4

All rights reserved. No part of this publication may be reproduced or transmitted in any form or by any means, electronic or mechanical, including photography, recording, or any information storage or retrieval system, without permission in writing from the publisher. The book is sold subject to the condition that it shall not, by way of trade or otherwise, be lent, resold or otherwise circulated without the publisher's prior consent in any form of binding or cover other than that in which it is published and without a similar condition, including this condition, being imposed on the subsequent purchaser.

Cover Image: *'Gust of Wind and Rainbow in Macha na Bo' by Niall Naessens – niallnaessens.com – Instagram @niall.naessens*
Cover Design & Typesetting: *Siobhán Hutson Jeanotte*

Printed in Ireland by Sprint Print

Salmon Poetry gratefully acknowledges the support of
The Arts Council / An Chomhairle Ealaíon

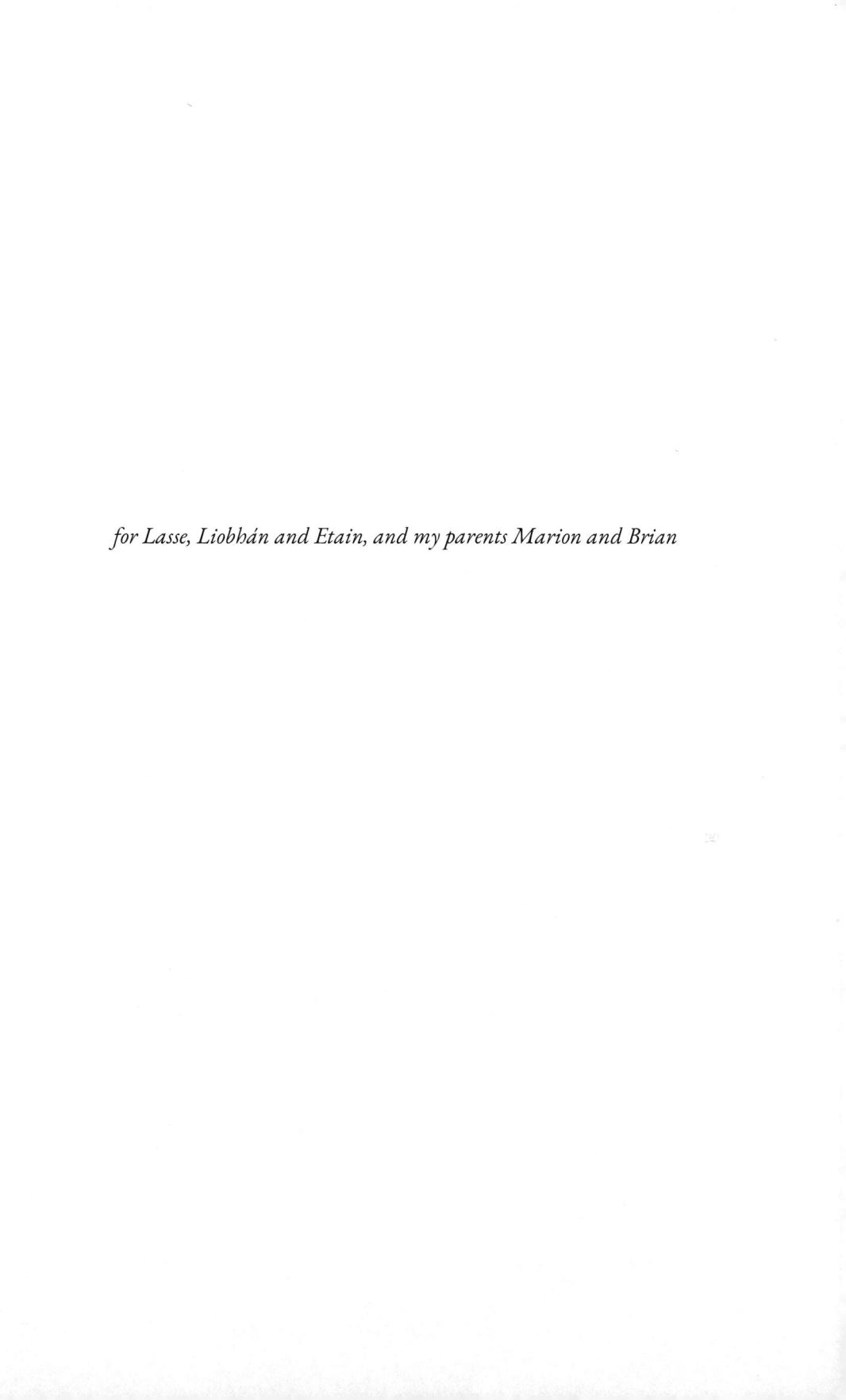

for Lasse, Liobhán and Etain, and my parents Marion and Brian

Acknowledgements

Thank you to the editors of the following journals and publications where some of these poems or earlier versions of them first appeared:

Banshee, *The Stinging Fly*, *The Irish Times*, *Poetry Ireland Review*, *The Poetry Bus*, *Two Tongues: Dánta Nua ó Chorca Dhuibhne* published by Ponc Press, and *Washing Windows III*, edited by Alan Hayes and Nuala O'Connor.

Thank you also to Mike Venner and Camilla Dinkel for their continued support through Dingle Bookshop and Ponc Press, to Words Ireland and Grace Wells for the best mentoring experience an emerging writer could have hoped for, to Dingle Writers' Group members past and present, with special thanks to Orna Dunlevy, to Féile na Bealtaine for their steadfast support of local writers, and to the brilliant and thriving community of poets here in Corca Dhuibhne – míle buíochas libh as an tacaíocht agus an comhluadar.

Thank you also to Jessie and Siobhán at Salmon Poetry.

Contents

I. *Here/Other*

Thin lines	11
The summer scarf	13
New gods	14
Field of Heads	15
Dreams tell you things	16
Magpies	17
Water	19
The damson tree	20
After the operation	21
Berry Fever	22
September	23
Cold snap	24
Gleann na nGealt	25
Gallarus Oratory	26
Nest	27
Running into my past	28

II. *Now/Then*

The Memory Bank	31
The Brickworks	32
Merrin's cure for warts	33
London Summer	34
The Singular Cloak	35
A bracelet of days	36
The hare skin	37
Vanishing act	38

III. *There/Here*

Letter home	41
The path to school	43
Columbines	44
Accident and Emergency	45
Deluge	46
Pearls	47
The school under the sea	48
The wave's lament	49
Scatterbrain	50
Chimera	51
Pilgrimage	52

IV. *Before /After*

My daughter leaves home	57
Questions	58
The rabbit	59
Macha na Bó	60
The brown bird	61
Before and after	62

About the Author	64

I

Here / Other

Thin lines

I crossed this line for the first time when things were moving too fast
and the wallop of a car
sent me spinning
into thin air
and set me
back down
on earth a
different
person

Afterwards the city trees marched dark
across the sky
the sun shone
too bright on a
gravelled
drive

College became lost hours
that slipped between my fingers
days turned into weeks
of not going to lectures

It took me a year
to find my way back
to the other side
of the line

It happened upstairs on a 65 bus
with the lights of Dublin
slipping away
beyond the bend
of Crooksling Hill
and my father sitting next to me pointing out The Plough

After that I watched where I walked

And when crows cawed
over snow white fields
lined with skeleton trees
and celandines gleamed
like fallen stars on the
banks around the house
and the dark beauty
of pennywort
stopped me
in my tracks

I knew the line
was thinning
and I took
a step
back

Now after years of walking this line
it's become a beautiful thing
I seek it out on coast roads
and on mountain ridges
and at crossing points

Sometimes I find that first line in my sleep
or walking Cuas na Nae
with my daughters
when the line
might disappear
altogether where
sea and sky
meet

The summer scarf

I left the house decked in my new
summer scarf. At the end
of the lane I met a woman dressed
in red, standing at the roadside
with a clippers in her hands
examining a tangle of brambles.
She looked at one bramble with utter
contempt and flung it onto the road.
When the man who delivered the coal
drove over it she wept.

'Why are you crying?' I said.
'It's just a bramble. That's all.'
She glared at me through dull red eyes.
'That's not the point,' she cried.
'That's not the point at all.
Oh why are you people so stupid?'
She pointed at the ditch
where the dark barbs crept,
sending out multiple arms to choke
damp tufts of grass, unruly vetch.

I left her and didn't turn back
until the rain came.
On my way home I met
a small black dog,
a cat missing his tail,
and two young girls, both long dead.
When I stood in to let a car pass
 a bramble snagged my scarf.
'Let go of me, you bastard,' I growled.

New gods

Year in, year out, from her windowsill
the virgin surveys the room.
Walls crack, damp blooms
and then one day a toilet appears,
along with strips of warped board,
rotten planks and picture frames
on the patch of grass outside.

Next week the house itself is gone.
Muck flows and sticks to tyres.
Muddy lakes collect, retreat.
Borne away on a mound of rubble,
the statue lands up in a neighbouring
field. Soil settles, silence falls.
Frost steals her blue robes.

The builders find the bottles under
the hearthstone – caked in dirt, but still intact,
there's one the colour of Sheep's Bit.
Plucked from the earth and rinsed with care,
they'll be displayed in the brand new hall
where the sun stalks in and decants their colour
onto sleek teak floors.

Field of Heads

Today I skirt seaweed, dodge dogs and rocks.
The late sun is low. It floods the whole strand.
There are others, like me, who walk back and forth
on this sickle of sand, this in-between place
where some say the living collide with the dead,
yards from where six hundred once lost
their heads in The Siege of Dún an Óir.

I walk, past the dunes, past Gortadoo,
past the soft field where bulrushes grow,
past the boathouse, my turning back point.
The path spins away, down a flax-lined lane.
Shhhhhhh the flax sighs, there are ghosts ahead.
The cliffs steal the sun. I am grey now, and cold,
like the stones of the wall I clamber across.
Behind me rooks gather on telephone lines
and caw out a warning, turn back, turn back.

When I come to a halt loss blooms from the soil.
I taste its dark form, in my mouth, on my skin.
The rooks keep their watch as I retrace my steps,
past the carved stone that won't let us forget,
past empty fields and dark shuttered houses,
past Gort na gCeann where their severed heads lay.
There's nothing to see now, just rocks and thin soil.
But back in my house on the hill I still dream
of twelve hundred eyes darkly blinking.

Dreams tell you things

The first time she conceived
she dreamt of a garden, lush and green,
where raspberries dripped darkly
from huddles of silver canes.

The fruit was ripe and sweet,
almost on the turn,
but she feasted on the berries
and savoured every seed.

With the ectopic she dreamt
her grandfather gave her an egg.
It was blue, too large for her hand.
But she took it all the same.

When she dreamt her mother was pregnant
at the age of seventy-eight
a friend warned "everyone in your dream
is an aspect of yourself."

The next night a baby visited
and whispered, "you know your friend?"
Listen to her. I'm coming. It's true.
Dreams tell you things.

Magpies

The day you leave
the drain backs up,
a print falls off the wall,
a robin gets trapped in the porch
in a frenzy of wings and fear.

And you drive on
and away,
shedding bits of us,
brightly coloured remnants
of all the things we've been.

I find a piece in the hall,
a faded scrap of your hat,
weathered from days
of digging
and walking the headland above.

You cross the Irish Sea,
drive all the way to Harwich.
I fill the house with flowers:
blue stars of borage;
unbowed spears of mint
newly gone to seed.

You find your feet in Arhus,
swim the Kattegat Sea,
drive across to Malmo,
just to see the bridge.
Back home the magpies chatter:
three for a girl, four for a boy.

I gather the pieces of us
and shove them under my pillow.
They cut my cheek while I sleep
and make me dream of trains.
Outside the magpies chatter:
One for sorrow, two for joy.

The day you come back
the house fills, sighs and settles down,
while the magpies watch
clackedy-clack from their perch
outside the porch.

Water

It started like a spring
whispering in my core,
gurgling, beckoning,
through night and early dawn,
till all around me, filling me, was water.

The water made me dazed,
drunken and content.
I stumbled through the months
growing heavy and replete,
with the water lap lapping deep inside.

My mother came to stay.
We talked and ate and ate:
asparagus in butter, tangy lemon pudding.
My belly bulged and swelled.
The water gathered weight.

Still, I wasn't ready for the wave when it came,
rushing me off my feet, flat onto my back,
hurling me right past the life I'd had:
my husband, the cat, my mother and I,
sitting on striped deckchairs
in the garden, side by side.
Its sheer force flung me clear onto a bed
where something warm and wet and blue
was tossed up on my chest
with a cry of 'It's a girl. It's a girl.'

The damson tree

Afterwards they gave me a book to read:
'To Baby Collins,
We wish we'd got to know you better.'
'To Baby Egan,
Miscarried, three months, four days.'
'To Baby Leonard,
We miss you so much, Mam and Dad.'

Later someone talked about planting a tree
and I pictured it, laden with bitter skinned fruit,
springing from a grave, to be cut down,
delimbed, and fashioned into pipes
that sang when they were played:
'I was baby might-have-been
 sucked from your womb
 by a white-gowned hospital team,
No. I wanted something more serene.

I waited for a day when the sky was high and clean
and then I let the idea of you float upwards and away,
until you were a distant speck, gone, no part of me.

But the next month you return, coming slowly in to land,
and I want to hold you, feather stroke your ever thinning skin
and examine you for signs of failure.

After the operation

They come in the night and early dawn
when a drip has slipped out or an iv bag
empties – first a golden-skinned man
in soft shoes who slides a cannula
into my vein in a single fluid move.
'Where are you from?' I ask him.
'South Sea Islands,' he whispers.
The guy who appears the second night is huge,
loose-limbed and vast with a blinding smile.
I laugh because we share the same joke –
morphine's a funny thing.

In the morning the dead people come,
one by one, out of the light, to murmur
their names and whisper 'remember.'
There is a boy, and an angry nurse
with bright red lips and raging curls.
When the place gets too full
I ask them to leave. Next day
their names are all gone. But sometimes,
years on, I see the boy's hair, in a leaf,
or a swathe of gold grass gone to seed
and his face, a question, an echo.

Berry Fever

for Caroline

The blackberries ripen early this year. I leave the house
laden with boxes and bowls and find women combing
hedgerows and fields, berry lust deep in their eyes.

You ring to tell me they've harvested the eggs.

I visit shadowed places I've never been before
and stumble across dark droppings outside some animal's den.
The air smells musky and unknowable. I run.

Meanwhile you sniff hormones, inject yourself.
At night a badger rampages through my dreams.
By day I snuffle my way through ferns and rotting grass.

Some berries are already on the wrong side of ripe.
Others have been annexed by a thin mucous veil.
These ones make my stomach turn. But still I cannot stop.

You will hear tomorrow if the eggs took.

Next morning in the mirror I am a foreign creature,
dark-eyed and wild with berry fever.
A deep white stripe cuts through the centre of my crown.

My lips are stained dark purple. My nails are ragged claws.
I smell the berries souring, in the kitchen, on the floor.
There are berries everywhere. There will never be enough.

September

The day is full of the usual things:
work, school, a trip to the shops,
small town traffic on the coast road;
Main Street's deserted
now the summer crowds are gone.

We get back home to find
September sliding across the lawn.
It slips into the kitchen where I'm slicing meat,
roams upstairs, checks out our beds,
examines the empty rooms.

We flick on rings, lights are lit. Potatoes
are tested, the table set. Outside moths
and daddy-long-legs gather. Hannafin's
horse whinnies dryly and night
washes up against windows and walls.

Cold snap

Outside the door
the world
is in a trance.
Ice packed flat tight
mirrors the sky.
Cars glide by
grazing ditches
with their wheels.
We coast on the edge,
sleepy-eyed, dulled,
lulled into calm
by this brand new cold.
In other places bitter
wars are being fought;
overcrowded boats
capsize; villages vanish
under mudslides.
And here we waltz
serenely on the rim,
step-step our way
through freshly
frosted grass,
tenderly prize free
sheets of ice
to smash them
on the ground.

Gleann na nGealt

Bay windows glow with fat christmas trees.
Plastic sleighs take flight. Squat santas roam front lawns.
On the road to Upper Camp snow starts to fall.

There's just the road and me
when Sliabh Mish looms into view –
immaculate, austere, in newly laundered white.

I stall. The car slides, and glides into a ditch.
When the mountain speaks its voice
is thick with earth and stone:

Forget the car. Do you want to know
what stillness is? Then come up here –
take the winding path the sheep have made.

Under a mound of stones you'll find a space where a king once lay.
Lie down. Stretch your limbs. Let the earth be your bed.
This is my gift to you. This is what stillness is.

A long time later moss slips into my ears.
Soil creeps over skin and inches between ribs,
flooding empty spaces that had waited to be filled.

Gleann na nGealt, a West Kerry place name, translates as Valley of the Mad.

Gallarus Oratory

A perfect up-turned boat outside,
inside it's rooted in stone.
This vessel will never
voyage an ocean.
In here the air is
still weighted
with prayer.
A slice
of
light
carves
the silence
in two and cuts
me through, dead
centre. For an instant
I am reborn – a quiver of silver,
a floundering fish, cast up on a dirt floor.

Nest

After you leave
I search the garden for a week.
I want to say we're sorry
and I wish I could go back,
to the quiet days before
the eggs were hatched.
We would lock up the dog
until the chicks were fully fledged,
keep the nest a secret
instead of showing it off.

But what if you asked me to rewind
to the day he came
and we gave him his name
and his bed in the porch –
or back to before that,
to the day we bought this field,
before we planted bricks in it
and built this house?

The images now refuse to stop,
spin back to the noisy home
where I grew up,
to my sisters and brothers in the Long Grass;
placing caterpillars back onto docks,
returning beechnuts to their shells,
sliding wet sods of turf into a bank,
releasing sticklebacks
and crayfish to the shallows,
retreating to our jumbled beds
to rest, limb to limb,
in our world of shared flesh.

Running into my past

I met her last week, on the way to Clothar Beach.
She was wearing that nice suede jacket she had
and she'd drunk a few shorts in the pub.

She asked me to come to Krugers to look out
at the Island and talk. I told her I was sorry,
that I couldn't, not the way things stood.

Later, when I was sleeping,
I heard her calling from the strand.
So I slipped out of bed and crept downstairs and got into my car
and drove
the half mile down.

When I got there she said 'look -
we're walking on air' and we ran
hand in hand, feet dancing on sand,
and when I looked down I saw the moon and the clouds
and my footprints stark and bare.

II

Now / Then

The Memory Bank

The first thing you find is an old tin box,
shoved in a corner, covered in dust.
Inside a tube of love-hearts glows
with the guilt of a nine-year-old thief.

Standing beside it is a worn high-chair.
Its canvas seat is torn.
A wooden spoon bashes out a long ago
tune on its cracked plastic table top.

Lined up in front of the counter rows of cribs
hold plastic dolls. One with a cap of shiny black hair
sits up and stares at you. Where have you been,
she asks, for the past thirty years or more?

The woman behind the counter
is wearing your first communion dress.
How much for the black haired doll?
you ask. I need it to put in a poem.
It's not for sale, she replies.
You can borrow the words. That's all.

The Brickworks

*Never set foot
in the place*
our parents warned,
but something drew us
to its metal girders
thin with rust,
the loose flap of tin
drumming out
a tup tup tap.

*Never set foot
in the place*
our parents warned,
but the dry pull
of red brick dust,
the elongated
hiisssss of a stone
cast into space
kept us coming back.

*Never set foot
in the place*
our parents warned,
but still we stayed
to play, to tightrope
walk on walls,
arms outstretched
like birds
about to take flight.

Merrin's cure for warts

That summer my hands
were covered with the things.
I was a toad, a monster, a beast.
When I met a boy I liked
I crossed my fingers behind
my back. I was the girl
with the witch's stamp.

My mother and I drove
the back road to Naas,
past the old couple who day in,
day out, sat in their glass
fronted porch, towards Sallins,
where the Fairy Tree stood,
and on to Merrins' place.

When we got there we found
Mr Merrin was dead.
He'd passed the cure
on to a daughter,
but she was long gone,
to the States. We could visit
his grave, if we wanted.

The headstone was draped
with scapulars and rags.
We said our prayers and my mother
drove home, pumped with
conviction behind the wheel.
'He was dead,' I tried saying.
'But the cure's not,' she said.

It didn't work. Not straight away.
It took them a year to vanish.
A year almost to the day.

London Summer

It is 1989. My brother and I,
and a friend whose name
I've almost forgotten
are sleeping on the floor
of Victoria Station.
After the coffee shops
and fast food joints close
the other people come:
young girls with shaved heads
dancing arm in arm,
boys in stonewashed jeans
with crudely drawn tattoos,
older men with faces
crosshatched into shade.
They root through the bins,
salvage half-smoked cigarettes,
devour out-of-date sausage rolls.

Night turns into days.
I do not find a job.
Instead I sit in the park
across the road
and listen to the trains
come and go.
My college friend
hooks up with a boy.
My brother gets work
on the sites. One day
I find myself back home.
At night as I lie in bed
the world presses in,
and back in Victoria Station
the trains come and go
and young girls
with shaved heads
dance across the tracks,
daring the train to take them down,
daring the train to slow.

The Singular Cloak

It is one of those tall days.
People on the street look elongated and lean.
The sun casts a sideways glance
at the walls of the Mansion House
and turns it into the Taj Mahal.

She sits on the 54a bus
wrapped in her singular cloak.
In front of her a mother hurls abuse
at her teenage son. Passengers purse their lips,
gaze at the Liffey, blink into the din.

The cloak is stifling.
She wishes she could breathe;
peel back the roof like a sardine can,
stick her head far, far, into the sky.

Instead she pulls her cloak
tightly round her neck – her singular cloak
trimmed with shiny black hair
complete with sharp barbs that keep the seat clear,
lined with thin lips that hiss 'don't come too near.'

In a garden they pass on South Circular Road
a woman hangs out her husband's clothes:
shirts wave, arms outstretched,
as the bus lumbers past;
kiss me, embrace me, they sigh.

A bracelet of days

You are making a bracelet of days
or bits of days
to take out in the half light
and know those other times were real.

The first stone threaded on is blue:
a dusky drive
through low flat fields,
that held the promise of home.

The second one is the gold
of candlelight in a night-time
chapel where four musicians
played.

The third is clear as water:
words plucked
from a poet's mouth
to flow into your ear.

You are making a bracelet of days;
moments stolen, frozen,
threaded into a talisman
to scare away those half-light days.

The hare skin

After my grandmother married
she never wore it again.
She left the hare skin in the family home,
folded in tissue, in a walnut wood drawer.

Years later my mother found it,
during a summer spent dreaming
and dancing to records
played on her aunt's gramophone.

She took the skin out and slipped it on,
bounded down narrow grassy lanes,
hind legs slapping the ground
as she fed from a drowsy cow.

She wore it until it crumbled to dust
and a whole world vanished with it,
of changeling babies, and ghostly tunes
playing on a dark hillside, to lure drunk men
into underground worlds never to return.

Now the hare is a mad March creature,
swerving through fading fields,
seeking what it has lost, ears cocked
for the sound of a long ago song,
playing in a hazy attic room, on and on and on.

Vanishing act

for Tessie

You are half the woman you used to be.
You sit in your fancy new jumper
like a freshly wrapped present.
When I put my arms around you
I meet only resistance; thin skin
and bone, not soft, warm flesh.

You are hawk-like, ancient.
You used to demand more space.
Are all these people sitting here,
are they half-people too?
That would explain their silence
while they try to remember themselves:
a strong arm here, a quick wit there –
days spent retracing a past littered with clues.

You are so small. In no time at all
I could pick you up and slip you into my bag.
I'd take care not to break you –
you are fragile, after all. I could take you home
and feed you, stroke your bony skull,
and maybe you would blossom, unfurl from where
you hide the twelve-stone country woman
who once picked mushrooms at dawn.

Meanwhile you plan your own vanishing act.
You set the scene: early morning,
a nurse bustles in. She pauses at the door,
takes in the unmade bed. All you've left
is the jumper, pale-pink beads around the neck.

III

There / Here

Letter home

Ordnance Survey
1867 Corca Dhuibhne

It is wet here, almost all of the time,
with a mist that seeps into nooks and crannies
and other unpleasant places.
The people of Dingle are surprisingly handsome
and do not resemble the Punch drawings too much,
although many sport rotting and blackened
teeth. But the language they speak
is like nothing you've heard,
littered with digs and jibes and curves.
And each tiny place has a name,
all of them sounding strangely
the same. For example: Loch, meaning Lake,
while Cnoc is a hill, they tell me.
And Cruach is – I don't remember,
though it drops from the mouth like water.

As for God, he's everywhere –
Dia Dhuit – *How do you do?*
And the devil too – th'anam 'on diabhal –
while history's tangled in every damn thing:
Gort is a field, Gorta is hunger,
and Gortaigh, believe it or not, is hurt.

The words get everywhere too.
A cleric I spoke to yesterday said
'there's a music in it that travels'.
He swore the people swallow
the language when they leave,
and it's only on some dusty
Boston street when they stumble
across somebody from home
that it shows its true colours again,
bursting up out of their mouths

in a verse, or stream of invective,
a little rough, but still able to fly,
from mouth to mouth and ear to ear:
Guttural – gearbh,
Unstoppable – gan stad,
Fíor. Which means true.
That's what he said. And I felt
the words bruise my lips like a kiss –
gearbh, gan stad, fíor.

The path to school

'What is the future, Mamma?'
We are clearing the path from our house
to the village. The air's alive with midges
and flies. I take a break from slashing back
nettles to ask where you heard that word.
'My barbies,' you say. You are not quite three.
'They asked me to come and fix things.'

Your sister's just started her Junior Cert year.
I used to walk this path with her. At first
we went right to the school wall,
then later she took to leaving halfway,
before they put the new pavement down
and we chose to forget all about this track.
But still it kept busy, filling itself.

'What is the future, Mamma,' you say.
The future is now, I tell you.
You chatter on as I cut branches down,
trying to clear all the way to the end,
to where I might find that other small child,
the one I left here just a short time ago
with the bag on her back, a few feet ahead.

Columbines

for Lasse

The house looks down at the vegetable patch
through a haze of willow and briars.
I break up the soil, pull sorrel and docks.
Columbines bow their heads,
a bright flood descended
from pilfered seed gathered from plants
in my parents' garden
over a decade ago.

I clear the weeds while bumble bees work
their way through the sea of flowers.
There are dozens of them, lazily buzzing
from bloom to bloom, fat bodies clumped,
punch drunk, under drooping bonnets.
I try a quick count but the bees never stop,
on to the next and the next flower and on.
I hear the soft thunk of a window being shut,
the swish of curtains being closed.

A mile down the road the sea rolls in.
A car breezes past. The day leaks warmth.
The bees work on and I crouch to watch.
I love their presence, their peacefulness,
their focus, their intent. I love the way
they accept these plants that only came here
on a whim. I love their sturdiness, their heart.
I love you, I say, I love you.

Accident and Emergency

A bloodied teenage boy curls up on the floor and sobs.
People look away. 'He needs to be seen', his mother says.

Medical dramas play out on two tvs. A young man in a coma dies.
A doctor has his skull sawed open and survives.

A clumsily bandaged old woman watches with one bright eye.
A dull-eyed baby in a stained sleepsuit pants in his father's arms.

We cling to our seats while outside the storm unspools;
flinging walls of rain at glass, ramming doors, rocking cars.

One young man gives up and dives into the night.
The rest of us stay put. We've come too far to go back.

The bandaged woman is summoned and disappears inside.
The weeping boy is brought in too, a parent on each arm.

At last a registrar calls my name and leads us into a room.
He tells me to blink, open wide, squeeze his hands in mine.

We wash up at x-ray and find the old lady, patched up with plasters
and tape. She smiles in recognition. Her hair is downy white.

Deluge

Water rushes down the hill behind the house.
It gathers on the ground when there's nowhere left to go,
pushes its way under the back door.
Dark stains bloom on the kitchen walls.
Cracks emerge. Plaster bloats. The chimney breast weeps.

A horse appears from nowhere in the neighbouring field.
At night his white coat gleams on the dark hillside.
By day he turns his rump to us and huddles against the ditch.
His broad back drips. His coat turns dull grey.
I bring him gifts – apples, carrots – I cannot stay away.

The rain falls and falls. The horse's ribs appear.
He tramples the food I bring into the sodden soil.
I picture him in my kitchen, his hooves thick with mud,
his flanks and shoulders shuddering with terror and relief.
I watch the rain steal his last trace of white.

He's barely visible now, even in daylight.
I mourn his muscled neck, his powerful limbs and glossy coat.
One day when I visit he is too weak to raise his head.
At night my ghost horse haunts me, a shade in a dark field.
You failed me, his phantom whispers. I needed more than gifts.

Pearls

for Antje

Winter's rain washes a century
of records clean off the charts.
Our neighbour, who's lived here for seventy years,
has almost had enough.
My daughters' faces turn pale grey
and I am a ship, cast adrift – my joints creak and groan.
One night I wake up not knowing who we are.
Stories pour out of my phone. Millions of people
take to the roads, marching miles through days
and nights, crossing seas in flimsy boats.

Our neighbour buys seed potatoes:
Duke of York and British Queens.
She will do what she does with them every spring –
leave them to sprout in a dimly lit room
and when the rain eases she'll plant them
in furrows lined with manure.
Over the weeks they'll shoot and leaf
into soft green rows, and when the flowers appear,
pale cream with an orange heart, she'll sink a fork
into the earth, flick the plant over and shake it off,
to uncover them, flecked with soil,
pale and contained, like dirty pearls.

She will serve them, gleaming with butter
on her mother's bone china
and she and her guests will agree they taste so different
depending where they've grown. And maybe
she will marvel once more at how she came here,
a girl washed up on a wave formed by the Second World War.
Maybe the years will unfurl back to the child she was,
lying in Glencree Infirmary with measles,
willing herself not to cry, trying not to think of her brother
and sister, her father and mother back in Bonn.

The school under the sea

In my dream there are no desks or chairs,
just hundreds of children, some in lifejackets,
others in simple cotton dresses, and more in fleeces,
to keep them warm during the overnight crossing.

Their clothes are sodden but they don't care.
They just want to know 'when will we be there?'
They tell me they can't go home.
They must wait for the boat to come.

A small girl climbs on my knee and asks for a fairy-tale.

When the sea steals my words she tells me instead
of spinning in circles while her mother sang
and the sesame biscuits her aunt used to bring.
She tells me of precious things.

The wave's lament

I am trapped here
in this in-between place,
not living but not dead.
I hunger for touch –
I swallow things: darkness,
people, the night, the moon.
My loneliness fills
the gulls' screams.
I am water,
cursed to wander,
searching for rest
in the cracks between rocks,
licking the ruin
of an island home,
gnawing jagged gaps
between cliff and path.
Listen to my tune.

Scatterbrain

This wind has un-tethered them all.
Just this morning she found the dog floating
a few feet beyond the hall door.
His eyes were white with terror. Later
a hen blew over the garden fence.
It's this wind. It does strange things
to the animals, her hair. Yesterday
she went for a walk and came back
all in a heap.
She barely knew herself in the mirror.
She'd swear that wind blew every thought
she'd ever had clean out of her head.
Sometimes she actually forgets he is dead.
Sometimes she thinks the wind
just blew him clean away –
clear across Brandon Bay.
'Come back,' she calls. 'Come back.'
But of course he never answers.
'How's she looking this morning?' he'd ask.
Well today the bay looks beautiful –
all cruel glitter and jewels. She misses him
when she loads the dishwasher. He was always
so bloody particular about where everything went.
She just doesn't know anymore.
She sometimes forgets what the things are called.
And the bed is cold. She uses two quilts most nights.

Chimera

Some people store loss in the weave
of their bodies, under a rib,
in the lock of their hips,
only to be walloped off course
years later by a burst of fleshy grief.

Loss is an opportunist, like the cells
my pregnant sister describes,
that dance from a foetus across the placenta
taking up homes in a mother's glands,
her spleen, her heart, her mind.

The cells start their journey just four weeks in.
I picture myself, my sisters, my mother,
flesh and bone temples to the children we've borne.
Might-have-been babies swell round my heart.
My head is home to multiple minds.

My thoughts aren't my own half the time. At night
I wake up in my daughter's dreams. My mother
is already there when I go to dial her number.
At dawn my unborn children sing of the paths
they have traced through the womb's night sky.

Oh mother, they sing, we are here. In this world
we inhabit you hold us tight, we sleep in your arms,
you whisper us songs, we travel the roads with
you, clasped to your heart. Oh mother, love is infinite here.

Pilgrimage

The tideline is frilled
with scallop shells
at the start
of the Saint's Path.
I fill my pockets
with crystals and stones –
for the journey, to keep
things at bay. I've lost things
along the way before.
Plenty of women
have walked this track,
not searching for saints
or the perfect shell,
just a hill
and a path to follow.
But today something
sounds in my gut –
a hum,
a tentative note.

At the last cross I empty
my pockets. The crystals
and keepsakes I gathered
have vanished, replaced
by a jumble of objects:
a hospital wristband says
sometimes things do not work out.
A medal of Gerard Majella
reminds me
that when something sacred
enters the room
it may leave
without explanation.
A DNA sample says
we are well matched.

A scalpel says science
is always a factor.
A bottle of pills says
vitamins matter.
A cool heart-shaped stone
in my chest dislodges
and air pours into my lungs.

IV

Before / After

My daughter leaves home

The bird is a white-bottomed boat
on the road above Dún Chaoin,
a shearwater drawn to the light
with no drop nearby to relaunch.

I park in the dark on the side of the road
and ring a woman who has done this sort of thing
before. She sounds sleepy.
'You just need to find somewhere with a drop.
That's quite something' she says, 'finding a bird like that.'
'This isn't the first time I've found one,' I tell her,
'I've just never launched them before.'
'It's a beautiful night,' she says. 'No wind.
If you don't do it now you'll have to keep it another day.'

Slea Head is all rock and stars and sea.
Every place I pull into is not quite sheer enough.
'They need the drop, to fall a bit first,' she'd said.
I finally find a spot below the cross.
Out of the car and standing in the dark,
the stars mark out a map above my head.
I turn off the headlights and open the boot,
clasp the bird tight into me, sharp shoulders and soft life,
find the spot where the sheer drop begins,
open my hands, cast it up and out.

Silence is what's left, and an empty space.

Even though I know it's no longer in the car,
I drive home with care and the same fear
I felt taking my newborn daughter home for the first time,
when I thought pulling a vest over her head might break her neck.

Questions

Driving through town after the first lockdown
I see him outside the funeral home.
He stands like he knows he belongs in this place,
a stranger from a country I thought was long gone,
where chilblains in winter were part of life
and babies lost were whispers
and clouds of smoke masked the smell of piss
and the threat of straying hands was accepted.

I picture him, listening to the radio in his kitchen,
deciding to come, draining his tea, fetching
from the wardrobe his black flannel slacks
and the jacket he bought when his sister passed.
I realise now I've been running
from someone like him for years,
casting off worn leather shoes as I went,
and hand-me-down jumpers that choked my child's neck
and thick layers of blankets that weighed me down
and paraffin heaters that singed my bare legs.

But today, seeing him here after all this time
I have only questions left:
does the weather scare you?
Do you ever pray?
What wakes you in the middle of the night?
Can potatoes suffer if they're planted too deep?
And that fear you feel when you see the leaves curl –
do you think it's the memory of hunger?

The rabbit

One day a rabbit appears outside,
gleaming black and white.
Weeks unfold and he comes and goes
like a ghost or magician's trick.
I do not know why he is here
or what he even means. But I know
he's not my mother – there is nothing
of her in him. He is nothing like her
in the way he moves
or in his fixed glassy stare, nor
in the way he charges the hens or
nibbles an apple with his back turned.

He lets my daughter stroke him,
eats tufts of sorrel leaves,
and stares at me unblinking
when I ask him what it means.
One day he doesn't come
and I tell everyone he's dead.
But the next night I watch him
face down a fox, coat glowing beneath
the moon. He is brave, I tell
whoever's nearby, my mother
was brave too. Why do you think
he's here, they ask me. What do you think it means?

Sometimes when I feed the hens
I ask them what it means.
They peck politely around my feet
and murmur ohdear ohdear.
I ask the robin who sang at the window
while the priest recited his prayers.
The robin releases a burst of song,
his small chest swollen with need.
In the car I listen to An Saol Ó Dheas,
in the evening I talk to trees –
Slithearnach, Fuinseog, Aiteann Gallda,
tell me, what does it mean?

Macha na Bó

The seed potatoes have arrived
You went so quickly
I never got to say goodbye
Outside the window that big Kerry sky
just pulled you up and away
You were gone long before
they hooked you up to the machine
long before the white puckered line
of your gallbladder operation
was revealed
Your mother has a scar – did she ever have surgery on her heart? Not your heart
I remember while you were away recovering we overfilled the chip pan
and we all ran into granny's room
yelling fire fire fire and she told us
to stop messing and get out
and daddy threw a bucket
of water over the cooker
and the whole kitchen
was destroyed
Yesterday
I walked up Macha na Bó
and everything had changed
The steep climb to the crossing
made me shake and up on the pass
clumps of red lichen glowed like clots of blood
My stomach hurts
Something's been unstitched
I used a stick for the first time
coming down and beyond the lake
the road unravelled
through rocky fields
bloated with rain

The brown bird

You say you don't believe in spirits Rest in peace you say
what does that even mean I tell you about one night in France
where a group of us saw a ball of light I tell you about the angry man's
voice in my head that same night when I lay in bed
how he only spoke French I tell you about my third eye
the one in the middle of my forehead how it opens when someone
I love is nearby That's just energy you say like a picture falling off a wall
when someone dies I tell you about the people my mother saw
when her mother was dying how they stood at the bottom of the garden
and waited I tell you how saying the words rest in peace
gives me permission to let go of my dead You need to believe in these things
you say So I tell you about the bird on the hill behind the house
how it calls all night a soft rolling churr and how I saw it sitting
in the garden twice last week I tell you I'm almost sure
it was a nightjar even though we both know
nightjars have never been recorded here before I tell you
about the world the two white ponies on the hillside have made
of gorse tunnels and pale green clearings and sweetscented piles of horseshit
where stonechats and hairy mollys and bog asphodel
and robins live I tell you about the handfuls of tiny fraughens
that shelter under the stern stalked ferns I tell you to look
see their dusky skin sniff the heather scent of them
I tell you tip a palmful into your mouth and taste
Fraughen Sundays stolen kisses the purpled lips of hungry children
the silent years of damp darkness that flood your mouth
and tickle your teeth now tell me you don't believe

Before and after

This line criss-crosses
millions of miles
slicing through borders
snaking forwards
until it reaches our doors.
We buy sanitiser
stock up on food.
The line forms circles two km wide.
We watch the news,
see numbers rise.
The sky clears.
The sun shines and shines.
Late at night
when nobody sleeps
we stand outside
under all those stars
and remember
how small we are.
Crawling into bed
just before dawn
cupped by the dark
with no cars on the road
we hear the earth sing.
Monarch wings hum
above the Gulf Coast,
the Blasket Sound
throbs a long note.
Next day we rub
the sleep
from our eyes,
haul out old bikes
from cluttered sheds,
wave to the people we meet.

Together we mark out
the line with our feet,
our bike wheels, our hands,
our eyes, our words,
our songs,
the walks that we take,
in this press pause
in-between place.

EMER FALLON grew up in West Wicklow and studied in Dublin before moving to the West Kerry Gaeltacht where she lives with her husband and two daughters. She has worked as a journalist, café manager and more recently as an environmental advocate, delivering environmental workshops to primary school pupils. Her poetry has been published in *Banshee*, *The Stinging Fly*, *Poetry Ireland Review*, *The Irish Times*, *THE SHOp*, and *The Poetry Bus,* and features in *Washing Windows III* and Ponc Press bilingual letterpress volumes *Two Tongues: Dánta Nua ó Chorca Dhuibhne* and *Port na bPúcaí*. She received an Arts Council Agility Award in 2022 to support her work writing and illustrating a climate themed children's story and is currently working on her second poetry collection. She also writes fiction.

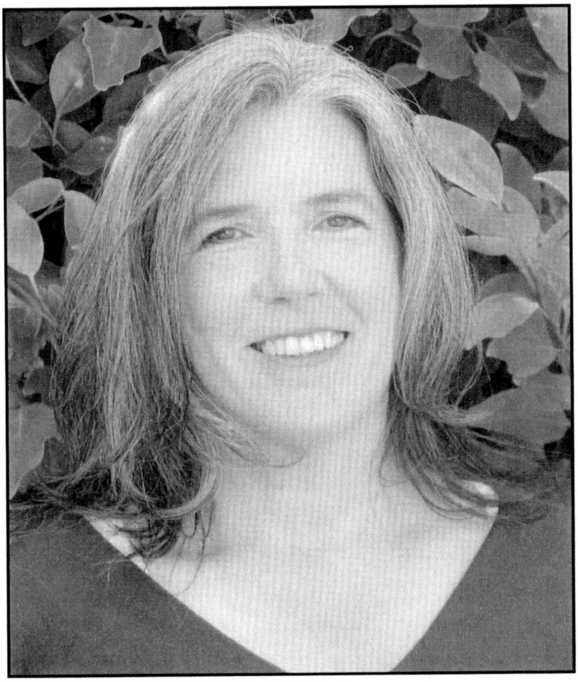